THE NATIONAL POETRY SERIES

The National Poetry Series was established in 1978 to ensure the publication of five collections of poetry annually through five participating publishers. Publication is funded annually by the Lannan Foundation, Amazon Literary Parternship, Barnes & Noble, The Poetry Foundation, The PG Family Foundation and the Betsy Community Fund, Joan Bingham, Mariana Cook, Stephen Graham, Juliet Lea Hillman Simonds, William Kistler, Jeffrey Ravetch, Laura Baudo Sillerman, and Margaret Thornton. For a complete listing of generous contributors to The National Poetry Series, please visit www.nationalpoetryseries.org.

2015 COMPETITION WINNERS

Not on the Last Day, But on the Very Last
by Justin Boening of Iowa City, Iowa
Chosen by Wayne Miller, to be published by Milkweed Editions

The Wug Test
by Jennifer Kronovet of New York, New York
Chosen by Eliza Griswold, to be published by Ecco

Scriptorium
by Melissa Range of Appleton, Wisconsin
Chosen by Tracy K. Smith, to be published by Beacon Press

Trébuchet
by Danniel Schoonebeek of Brooklyn, New York
Chosen by Kevin Prufer, to be published by University of Georgia Press

The Sobbing School
by Joshua Bennett of Yonkers, New York
Chosen by Eugene Gloria, to be published by Penguin

TRÉBUCHET

TRÉBUCHET

POEMS BY

Danniel Schoonebeek

THE UNIVERSITY OF GEORGIA PRESS   ATHENS

Published by the University of Georgia Press
Athens, Georgia 30602
www.ugapress.org
© 2016 by Danniel Schoonebeek
All rights reserved
Designed by Erin Kirk New
Set in 10 on 13 Adobe Garamond Pro
Printed and bound by Thomson-Shore, Inc.
The paper in this book meets the guidelines for
permanence and durability of the Committee on
Production Guidelines for Book Longevity of the
Council on Library Resources.

Most University of Georgia Press titles are
available from popular e-book vendors.

Printed in the United States of America
20   19   18   17   16   P   5   4   3   2   1

Library of Congress Cataloging-in-Publication Data

Names: Schoonebeek, Danniel, author.
Title: Trébuchet : poems / by Danniel Schoonebeek.
Description: Athens, Georgia : University of Georgia Press,
    [2016] | Series: The National Poetry Series
Identifiers: LCCN 2016020561 | ISBN 9780820349923 (pbk. : alk.
    paper)
Classification: LCC PS3619.C4538 A6 2016 | DDC 811/.6—dc23
    LC record available at https://lccn.loc.gov/2016020561

CONTENTS

TRÉBUCHET

These poems were written to land you on a government watch list.

And published at $19.95 paperback (hardcover edition
unreleased) by an impostor of Faber & Faber of 320 South Jackson Street, Athens
inside a warehouse formerly occupied by six pinkerton deserters
in this year of our lord 2016 the year of the so-called "accident."

Or maybe to throw a brick through the wall of the White House
and no note attached is their business.

These poems come pepper-sprayed for your health with dirty words
particularly on pages 7, 19, 29, 66, and 70
and were written by D. Schoonebeek
an oftentimes troubled and defamatory young girl
living among the worst generation of profiteers in balaclavas
and who keeps herself violent through love.

Or maybe to start a riot inside the insurgence
inside of the skirmish is their business.

Their weight is 9.356 ounces,
they will travel 732 feet in 12 seconds when fired from a trébuchet,
their burning temperature is Fahrenheit 451,
and they were printed in these United States by
McNaughton & Gunn of Saline, Michigan.

Or maybe to smuggle the anthem back inside the chrysanthemum is their business.

On the day of its publication this book

would buy you 4 loaves rye peasant bread,

8 white bootlaces,

1 liter vodka filtered through cheesecloth,

5 lbs. goose feathers,

0 theater tickets,

7 single rides on Manhattan-bound bus lines,

3 boxes baby diapers,

11 yards steel chain,

0 paintings, 5 cartons eggs,

or a starred review in *Publishers Weekly*.

What else do you expect

for $19.95?

No really: what do you demand of your money.

What is the *function* of police?

Their International Standard Book Number

is nine seven eight

zero eight two zero three

four nine nine two three

and this is the same number of school shootings since 1986.

This is the same number of school shootings since you were first broke.

This is the same number of school shootings since you were last fucked.

This is the same number of school shootings since you lost the use of your left.

This is the same number of school shootings since the so-called accident.

This is the same number of school shootings since Flight 370 vanished.

This is the same number of school shootings since god said I defect.

This is the same number of school shootings since you laid down your weapons.

These poems will offend a number of people who will refuse to ignore them,

some of them people with *fathers*,

fathers in law or fathers on Capitol Hill,

and men and women of influence with fathers of money in Iowa.

Their commercial potential is laughable,

the Big Five publishers will spend zero money printing these poems,

zero money ordering cured meat for the book party,

the ruling class will read them but only on days

when a family member is assassinated or during nationally televised tragedies,

and they will tell you the middle class is vanishing,

but the middle class will beat itself to death with this book,

the middle class will call this young girl a woman of hatred of men,

the middle class will critique her,

the middle class will call her a national treasure,

the middle class will market her,

the middle class will interrogate her about her sex,

they say the middle class has vanished

but it's the poor of this country who should rear up and throw books of poetry

through the walls of the White House

and no list of demands attached.

These poems are dedicated to no man or woman who's yet been born,

to the slugs that will never leave your gun,

to milkmen Miss Universe snake oil salesmen

Russian volleyball champions grave diggers

bribed congressmen waste managers astronauts

deserters zookeepers mega-millions lottery winners

knife collectors ex-military tax evaders careerists

doomed politicians musicologists bread and butter men

buskers anti-defamation lobbyists government shills

bad feminists okay feminists slander enthusiasts postal workers

wall street propagandists gunrunners unfamous poets

advice columnists javelin throwers failed nuclear

warhead designers beauty school dropouts

spam writers cocktail artisans viola wunderkinds

Brazilian crust punks mall cops secret service men

taxidermists web hackers hypnotherapists stunt actors

card sharks bible thumpers porn stars manchildren

fire eaters lumberjacks bodyguards and whistleblowers

conspiracy theorists hijackers children born without throats

hung juries and hangmen and whomever death will not love.

If these poems don't throw themselves through your windows please burn them.

If you are the same person building himself a ham sandwich

inside his living room after you finish them

please shoplift every edition of this book you can find

please tear out the pages

and please burn them to warm your house through the winter.

The time of writing books that don't send us to jail is dead.

Drinking vinho verde under the harvest moon and puttering our lines is dead.

Asking yourself and asking yourself why a poem is the enemy of money is dead.

If you will leave this book on a wood slat and gaping down at the world

please throw it on the floor instead.

Or instead please burn it.

Instead fire it out of a trébuchet at the White House.

This book was written to terrify the fucking.

Like the last poems you read before the hostile takeover.

Like the first lines you speak when the plane disappears.

This book was written to break the back of the sawhorse between you and the police.

A book like the earth you might salt if you warred against you.

But then one of them gets the idea to build a building.

A building whose ruins,
when they fall—

they will pile up more beautifully than the building itself.

And one by one they tell them to build new monuments,
new gasworks and watchtowers,

new barriers, new thrones, and new battlements,

and they will,
over thousands of years—

they will become these beautiful ruins all by themselves.

•

Now I can't tell you what end that journey was toward.
But I can tell you I am its end.

(Rain, gunfire, crows)

A law of ruins, they called it.

TRÉBUCHET

NACHTMUSIK

If the nightcrawlers sing through the loam tonight will I join them

A boy who was born
with the blown out voice

of a legendary
backwoods catcaller

& built his fortune on the scalp of his Anna

in the podunk
vistas of nowhere

•

Will I join them the nightcrawlers
if they chew

through the soil & sing

& gasp for pink dew
& meat

like the wood that gasped through my pink when I started my teething

•

If they sing will she barb them my love in her eating dress

so *schlank* my Anna

married off

like a heath dweller

& into the arms

of her reddleman

Can she hear them the fish hooks still ring

like our teens

when we were hated & ate our handful of worms like the song bragged

.

It's the law

Rome told me

I was gassed next slung to a hinny next chased from town with my hands tied

I woke & was ancient

next gutshot

next slack

next saw

the tramps sleeping

in Bank of America

& dressing the sores in the heat the earth let escape her

It was a menagerie of tramps
like a handful of nightcrawlers

& dreaming they're eating
themselves back inside her

•

But have you met my new love
the sylph

drunk like a war hero on Armistice Day & flaunting her Croix de Guerre

She smells the song
the nachtmusik

I sing when I'm trying to touch her

& cracks her legs
her eyes for the sailors

"Her mound"

"She's my lowing sinkhole"

•

His face that was armor it's chinked like a cutting board

he sullies

my catwalk down Broadway she lows

(love ignores love

ignores & goes

rogue)

My inamorata the sylph in her crinoline skirt & her fishnets

I belong

in this Canyon of Heroes she lows

catcalled & flogged

like white meat

& hornswoggled

she hums to her mouthful of worms

•

Is this our spoils boys

for sacking Rome

I hum to my mouthful of worms

I was legendary

in my hey

in my pink

with my fortunes hung low for my Anna

You look at me now

I'm paler

than Ovid

& punching the earth with a trake & cleaning

your love from my hooks

like a dusting of misfired snow

•

& Anna the worms

can we join them the worms

who sang you off to your reddleman

& Anna your fortune

is your fortune

in Bank of America

& Anna the tramps

do you feed them your meat & your spoils

do you feed them the loam they dream they eat back inside you

& Anna the sores

tonight in your crinoline I see you dressing your sores

I see you cleaning my love from your trake

& Anna the nightcrawlers

we're so far from our heath

& will we join the nightcrawlers beneath the gutshot columns of Rome

FIFTEEN ANSWERS OF THE KING TO HIS QUESTIONERS

Yes I tasted my wife taste   the go-devil

they lowered   from heaven & I saw

the white handkerchief   they hung down

from heaven to earth   & I surveillance'd

three barrels: one liquor   one oil, one milk

& heard the first whisper   *I boil to black*

& heard the black whisper   *I boil to milk*

& heard the last whisper   *the milk boils all*

by itself yes I watched   the old warlander

she was lording me   over her colt & a black

grouse was present   he was tearing out

grass by the roots   & weaving this grass

in his fetlocks   this young horse was neighing

Yes I tasted my wife taste   the liquored

lie down on her shit heap   taste the curs

come to sniff   at the womb in stockades

in the courtyards   I tasted the Catholics

they begged   to kneel down for a century

& I saw the horse   they prophesied I'd leave

my wife for: she had four heads   & each one

was grazing on clover   but only one leg

to sustain her yes I tasted   my wife taste

a worry rock no   a warchest of pearls no

a merit badge   & I saw the pigtail of smoke

that shook them   from heaven to earth

& I saw the chow line   & the rich in the chow line

& deserters were   handing out paychecks

demerits, bonuses   false teeth or flour

Tell me where   is my bonus said the desert

& the sacks   were picked clean yes I tasted

my wife taste   these stones with beards

like the devil's   they rolled down from heaven

& goose-stepped   when they tasted the earth

& three women I loved   from my youth I saw

weaving daisychains   & smearing each other's

wrists, each other's chests   with raw honey

& crowning themselves   with their chains

& pressing to steady their prayer   their wrists

to the earth   & I saw many henchmen

with horseshoes for eyes   with god's veins

in their barrels   with shoes filled with salt

& this is the devil's workforce I said   & I put them to work

THE DANCING PLAGUE

But who was the woman who lived in the kingdom behind the barrier.

There are those who will tell you she was the wife of every man in the village.

And one night while her husbands were finishing their day at the gasworks,

the woman was boiling oats for her only child,

a young girl who'd amassed a beautiful collection of spoons in her life,

each one given to her by one of her mother's husbands.

And this same night the young daughter died.

And the woman buried the daughter with her spoons in her pockets.

Come daybreak the hostiles appeared at the barrier with ice in their beards.

"To hell with Pax Americana," they said.

And they camped outside the wall that night chanting war cries.

You say you want to know the names of the war cries that survived history.

"Wheel the gun carriages up to the barrier of the empire of husbands."

"Our first word is ruin and our next word is value."

There are those who will tell you the hostiles carried on like this for some weeks.

Until one night the dead daughter led them behind the barrier,

through a tunnel she'd dug in the earth with her spoons.

It was thus the hostiles made it their business to burn everything.

They burned the village crops and the distillery.

They burned the apothecary, the potash mine.

Black soot fell on the livery and they burned the livery too.

And there's another war cry that's since survived history:

"Tonight like god's scalp in your kingdom behind the barrier

our burning makes snow and ends nowhere."

You say, where were the village husbands while all of this was happening.

There are those who will tell you they were working their jobs at the gasworks,

and when they heard the bullhorn roar in the watchtower

they were smoking cigarillos and pacing the floor of the gasworks.

And the roar of the bullhorn had a strange effect on the husbands,

who each began daydreaming of his wife at home in the village.

The first husband thought: "the taste of the breath of my wife,

it's like saying the word *houndstooth* to myself in the dark."

The next husband thought of her letting her hair down in front of a vanity,

and smearing her blue eye shadow onto her fingers,

and plucking the stray hairs and flyaways off her head.

The next husband thought of her saying, "I'm correcting god's blunders,"

when he asked her why she wears all this foundation on her face.

Another husband thought: "quitting time is worthless to me

so long as the work I do in the gasworks makes me think of my wife's jawbone."

And all together the husbands said: "the jawbones of my wife,

they beat both the same, like when I miss a train leave the kingdom,

and all I can see is the pistons beating away in the smoke."

And when the hostiles entered the gasworks the husbands were dancing.

And you say you want to know the words the hostiles spoke when they entered.

There are those who will tell you they said this: "don't quit dancing."

"There's a penalty for an empire that believes it can survive itself," they said.

And so they pointed their war clubs at the husbands,

and they said don't quit, don't quit dancing on the floor of the gasworks,

and they bludgeoned to death the husbands who refused to keep dancing,

and one by one the husbands fell dead on the floor of the gasworks,

each one dancing himself to death at the hands of the hostiles.

And this dancing took many deaths.

But you say where was the wife who lost all her husbands this day.

There are those who will tell you she was hiding the last of the cheese in a boot.

She was rolling up the deed to her house in the village.

She was picking up her daughter's violin and stuffing the scroll in the violin's f-hole.

She was fleeing for the wall when she was stopped by the hostiles.

Dance, said the hostiles, and they pointed their war clubs at her skull.

And these war clubs had a strange effect on the wife,

who began daydreaming about a man who wasn't her husband.

She thought of cutting his hair in a sunflower patch in the village.

The time should be dusk, she thought, and the shears,

they should flash once in her hands like a scythe.

She thought there should be two swarms of no-see-ums,

one smoldering around each of her hands.

And she'd tilt back the head of the man who wasn't her husband.

And she'd oil his throat with the badger brush in her hand.

And he'd smell the sandalwood lather she worked in the bristles.

And he'd smell the eau de cologne on her neck when she leaned in close.

And she'd shave his throat with the blade of a balisong.

And the woman thought each time he moaned when she stroked him

a dragonfly should dance from his mouth.

And he'll moan until the dragonfly quits dancing, she thought.

And I'll dance around his throat all night like a lantern.

"Because a war club doesn't taste like a war club," she said.

"It tastes like my husbands all breathing at once."

She spoke these words with a hole in her skull in the snow.

And the smoke coming out of the hole was her thoughts.

And her body lying there in the village square was so beautiful

the hostiles began to dance on either side of the body.

And they danced, and they danced, until they too fell dead in the snow beside her.

THIS NEVERENDER

There's a saw discontinues the loved who are void I have seen it.

I have seen it as I have seen from the mess hall

their seventh-degree burns rise again.

As I have seen in the bagnio my consumption it rises again.

This existence in which I blame god on the tree line through which you no longer intrude.

This ending in which I withdraw myself from your banks but I've seen it.

When I return from you like a failed occupation.

And I stalk your geese who make laughingstock of my enemies.

And into their villages.

And the clothes I wear gasoline.

There's a love that persuades you I've seen it:

beating to death a politico ·

on the steps of the White House for another half century

will equal a riot

on behalf of the strange who were loved

who are void

but I've loved it.

I have loved it as I have loved the mobs who are coming to disfigure my liberty.

Who say a stranglehold's coming for me

that cares least for my throat.

And this existence in which I blame money on the lowland into which you won't cloud.

And they tell me god's wealth is my throat within reach but I've seen it.

I have seen it as I have seen you bed down in a pauper's grave

and the worms tell you god is sketch.

I have seen them announce

the airstrikes are here for your mess halls

but I can't say if I felt the compunction.

If I did I was young.

Or if I did I was you.

And god's wealth was my throat within reach.

COYOTE TACTICS

In a country not seen by daylight.

Unburned fuel between you and the fire.

Zero communication between you and the supervisor.

Uninformed on strategy, tactics and hazards.

Weather keeps getting hotter or drier.

In a country not seen by daylight.

Attempting a frontal attack on the fire.

Terrain and fuels make escape to safety difficult.

Instructions, assignments not clear.

Wind increases or wind changes direction.

In a country not seen by daylight.

Fire not scouted or fire not taken.

Unfamiliar with weather's influence on behavior.

Cannot see fire, not in contact with anyone who can.

Safety zones and escape routes not identified.

In a country not seen by daylight.

Building a fire without building an anchor point.

Or building a fireline with a fire below.

Or seeing a number of fires across the fireline.

On a hillside where rolling debris can ignite fuel below.

In a country not seen by daylight.

And falling asleep near the fireline.

C'EST LA GUERRE

But if I see one more shred of pink rust come peeling off the face of this warehouse tonight.

With my bouquet of railroad ties that I plucked from the Union Pacific who'll witness me.

When I've found the man who named the road on which you grew up and defaced him.

And wearing his father's crushed suit and his cufflinks and I fire your name in his furrows.

When I've poured his mother a whiskey and coffee and beerback I'll learn her our myth.

We come from low country with deer ticks in our blood is that what they're selling you.

In search of the black horse who spits on the hay and the barley and hunger strikes.

Who lost the blue horse he loved and he'll die with his eye on the wood where she fell.

Well I fire your name in the furrows tonight for the ones who refuse to survive themselves.

Who say every five seconds the nations of dead they tell me my job is assuage them.

And every five seconds when I tear out their stitches I tear them out five seconds long.

It is you with the planks of rotting-down barns in your arms I am barreling toward.

It is you from the jackshit connivances of yesterday's scofflaw patrol I will kidnap.

And who will say amen if I fell one more empire that was raised from a handful of litter.

And who will help quit our mothers who will not quit treading the rafters of savagery.

And who will carry our fathers from the ditches where they crashed their radio flyers.

With a bouquet of railroad ties in a crushed suit I will field you this question come winter.

In the apocryphal gossip of sea kings my face is scrimshaw like they've never witnessed.

He sunk himself like a dreadnaught into the sea to landmark her joy is that what they say.

And who will witness me if I'm one page in a long book of ways to say no with no ending.

And if I come to your door come winter in crushed suit with the stitches to prove you.

COLD OPEN

It was the thought that—

if you could watch, if I could leak to the public the *film* of when I needed to reach you—

that would be one way.

•

From a little-known bluff overgrown last summer with wildflowers,

if you could watch a family of turkeys,

a mother and 162 poults,

if you could watch them abandon their roost on the lowest branch of a cottonwood tree,

and lugging 163 tow cables behind them when they departed,

if you could watch them dragging the tree through a field overgrown last summer with

   tanglehead grass.

And discarding the yellow tree pitilessly across the rails of the Sunset Limited,

which was carrying that day exactly 162 passengers west to their sentencings.

It could be one way, I kept telling myself, to awake in summer when everyone's sentenced

and film myself shut of those dead to me.

If the lights came up on my train in a field overgrown last summer with tanglehead.

If we could slow to a halt in front of the yellow tree obstructing our path.

There could be a smash cut,

an establishing shot of the bluff where you knelt cutting wildflowers,

and off-camera the cottonwood could start hemorrhaging yellow termites,

if you could see the mites glowing yellow having drunk the yellow blood of the tree.

If I could leak to you what the camera work couldn't—

in a hand-me-down suit

an unsavory man

he's inside a renaissance cherry casket,

and the casket's buried eight feet beneath the Sunset Limited's engine room,

and the casket's rigged on the inside with a hand-crank generator,

with Christmas lights in five colors,

if we leaked red first then blue,

green before we leaked orange, last yellow,

the light of which illuminates the interior of the casket enough for the man

(he's alive)

to watch his face decompose in the mirror that's rigged to the ceiling,

if we could cut to the sentence handed down to the man many years ago,

that any unsavory man is a man who should watch himself die.

If there was a slow zoom on a woman's hands typing eight words in first class,

a slow dissolve to a child in coach,

if he fingers a text that says *don't change for you,*

don't change for me, if there's no ellipsis, no period at the end,

if he doesn't need to ask who it's from.

From a little-known bluff you could stand up with a fistful of wildflowers.

You could watch the faces of 162 passengers darken unannounced

as if from a lightning storm.

If the cottonwood could stand up from the rails and dust off her own blood herself.

Resume her cold work, untangling the grasses.

If you could watch the train resume its terrible campaign for the west.

Unseen for you I could stay buried here,

beneath 162 suitcases with the rest of the stowaways.

INTERNS

Do us scofflaws belong here us scoured and laughingstock

who drag up

our work sacks

our brickbags yes trowels

our mortar

us women whose bellies are sag low

and scuff

and leave a white trail where they drag cross the floor

Do our husbands assigned us wake up in the trenches

and hear us salute

our nimrod our blind man

(who carved us

our plot is who fired

our furnace)

and our blessing's our work and our building's our blessing

•

Letter the peregrine delivers my husband each morning reads death to the boss

because "boss"
means you watch him

when he shears
my wool in the break room

and burning his name in my flanks you won't
doubt I'm livestock

A boss is like god
only smarter a boss means you hear him

he settles
my name in the ledger

and signing his name on my timesheet he writes
"I'm babel" in chalk

His signature doesn't it look good to eat just like peasant bread

All the holes

nibbled through

in his yeast

all his crusts

good and stale

for my soups

A boss means

the leather

that holds up my slacks

he scratches

his name there the pennies

I place in my loafers

that shine

on the tongue

It's death to the boss because "boss"

means he authors

the front of my paycheck and husband believe me I witness him

A fresh coat of flour

his name

on the crumbs I sneak home

His name is the mouse god when the mouse god abandons his hole

And husband why

is my name

always looks

like the last

train through

town hit it

Or better yet

our blind

nimrod's chariot

And answer me husband will the boss sign me too

When you answer me husband

will the boss sign you

When she cries will we see

in chalk

in her mouth

the boss

on our child's dead tooth

Let's pray he signs her with fire and we all call her gospel

Let's pray on my cable

back south

to the trenches

I graze

past the boss

on his way to the heavens

.GIF

Waste, do you know the word. Often it comes at night when I'm auditioning for the part of myself. When I'm mouthing the name of a politico, or fucking myself, or wondering why I carry on being American. Waste means whatever waste wants. In the middle of my life I searched for my name in the engine. I'm not dead links and leaks and zero results. Gospel I told myself. I wrestle the ancients and yell their names when I'm blackout. I unleash myself on myself and I fuck the crow from my songs. But waste means here comes the shepherd's crook. Ask me anything I'm the bellwether nobody brands. Waste and my telegrams of the cockscomb and teaspoons and my face in the cities I love they will vanish. I've failed to convince myself to subscribe to myself. Or I stand before the wall on which nothing's written. Waste means I'm following. Or I came here to waste in this box and everyone called it life. Waste finds me new addresses, new names every day. A red name, a green name, turned orange. From these three hooks the world is hung. The world which won't bend to the wind and waste means traffic, select invitations. Waste means I'll interview Salt, the town drunk whose father guards waste for a living. "One day two dozen years ago he came home smelling like shit." Are you like my father, Salt asks, do you oversee the river of waste to make money. Waste this river of carp and scumbags, it's peasant bread with the crust come alive. When you catch me disabling my family filter. "Shit is definitely one of the top three smells I think of when I think of my father," Salt tells me. The others? Ask someone else, waste the others. In the middle of your life and we're sorry nothing matched your search. He says I fired my gun into the river and nobody published it. The birds will sing none of it back. Waste is you stop telling stories. "Gospel," Salt writes me. I've thought of my father below me. Guarding his river of shit when I flush down the hole. Waste and return to the engine. When I fire my weapon I audition for the part of myself. Waste creates my page in the encyclopedia of waste. No one has met my waste yet, not even me, but my waste starts the bidding at zero. "I've only seen the place from the road," Salt writes me. "You've seen it too." My father's kingdom, and he defends the river of waste until it reaches the sea. Waste it's none of my business, waste is to hell with the scene. On these two hooks you hear waste chanting encore. Waste wants my chronology spread out like waste on a wipe. My father was born and fired his gun into the river and two dozen years now he watches the shit floating past him. Waste of a nut, waste of a rearing. Waste of a man, get rid of yourself. Delete your waste then return to the engine to scour. Audition for the part of your father in the film where he leaves you for waste. Or everyone wastes on my wall on the day I was born now. I've failed at waste but I've died, is that not also a triumph. I loved a politician, I've wasted another. Auditioning for myself, will I waste in the engine and result in myself. Father he curses the waste floating past. Will I mouth the name of a politico, waste of a cheekbone, tonight while she floats down the river. A raft and the suitors of waste on her arm. Foie gras smeared like waste on their teeth. Toy soldiers and dead cats and wedding rings in the river. My father steering the raft with his pole. "John my father," Salt writes me. On this one hook the world is hung. Waste of a name. Waste of a name I never made for myself. Waste has me flagged for removal, wants my history. "I've wondered," Salt tells me: could I break into the tunnels tonight and waste the toll collector. Bury his name and his pole. Unfollow him. And write my father, the waste king, write his name on the throne instead.

RUSSETS

We planted potatoes   because potatoes go blind

Potatoes lose skin   when they stew in the crock

Scalped her we pulled the hair   we said mother

mother your raw Irish skull   why is it so full of weeds

And plucking a lash from her face   mother your face

why do father's Dutch tulips   still grow here

But now we meet on the bridge   and talk crops

And we meet like a screw   meets a ratchet brace

The bankers they tell us   money's none of our business

The brokers they want us   to sleep in the breakers

The police when they read us   the rights to our poem

they forget who barricades who   with a sawhorse

Will you beat me to death   with Abraham's beard officer

Should we wait for politicos   to throw us a war

and we'll all go invisible   and click not attending

And when you drive us away   and white bullhorns

should we buy ham and rotgut   in the capital city

should we trade our shit-dirt potatoes   skin and all

should we trade her tulips and lashes   trade mother

and falter before the banks   and demand a meal

We demand ham god damn it   and not glazed neither

We hate potatoes   History every day it's potatoes

and this Sunday   like blight in your sculpture garden

we'll dress our table   in your warhawk's shadow

How do we look Manhattan   with our throats swoll shut

no peasant bread for this boy   no table crumbs for that boy

but grinding our flint corn   on the curb beneath your boot

and tossing the flour   on the heap the Greeks left us

We boil our soup for our lady   of refusing to die ugly

We bake bread for our lord   of kissing a cop on the mouth

Already I heard the newscaster call it   "the American fall"

and I too would like to plummet   and still be a nationalist

And tomorrow when I sew   my Madison Ave face back on

And Mortimer my boss   he calls for the language budget

he'll tell me that money   is how well you talk crops

and his face like potato skin   and it stews in the crock

Have you finished he asks me   "my language budget"

Have you got my quote   have you tendered your letter

Brooklyn Bridge you look good   stuck in his throat

like the tusk of a mammoth   slow-basting in soot

Mortimer I wonder how many times   like my bank card

will the sky be denied   Mortimer how many russets

will be born and go blind   before the country is potash

Your deadline is coming he says   and guns me down with his finger

Fall it comes like a barricade   and you owe me my language

CHORUS

Saw a world was the straw-bale house

I spent

my life building

& caved in on herself

once a shift

whenever my auger brace

finished her

was to be

(& the god in the herringbone

hard hat

decreed this)

the legacy of the legacy

of my legacy's

legacy's legacy

POEM WITH A GUN TO ITS HEAD

This appeal for the allocation of government surplus money to pay for the execution of the following work, which will be staged in a warehouse marked for demolition and of the author's own choosing, will be ventured via submission of the above-named work itself, a poem oftentimes troubled by an undetermined malaise, entitled "Poem with a Gun to Its Head," in which the author, 23% of an unsavory person named Danniel Schoonebeek, 30 years of age and rumored to be a resident of an unincorporated village populated solely by a fringe network of radio hijackers (and hereafter known as "the client"), puts forth the following terms, necessarily on the grounds that, quote, "already a new death is here to bargain with you," and, quote, "already this new death," in the client's own addendum, is, quote, "*already* already rebranding itself in your garden": (1) that the client will be provided with a scrubbed work desk, scoured preferably by a machine that is capable of manipulating either steel wool or sandpaper in what will henceforth be known as its "claws"; (2) that the client will be provided with one single red ballpoint pen and a roll of third-generation organic toilet paper priced at $4.67 per unit, on which the client will undertake the writing of a poem entitled "Poem with a Gun to Its Head"; (3) that the rules, toxicity, patrolled borders, whiteness, stench, duration, blurriness, foul language, malice, flammability, intolerability, nerve, subject-verb disagreement, and potential for insurrection of this poem will be determined under the following criteria; (4) that the client's childhood friend, Nicholas J. Frandsen, a platoon sergeant of the United States Marine Corps (who will have served no less than two tours of Iraq, and wearing his Marine-issue fatigues, and rumored to have once beaten two men unconscious with his bare hands, necessarily on the grounds that they tipped their waitress below 5% on a bill of $117), will aim and press a military grade AK-47, purchased illegally with money earned via time served in the U.S. Marine Corps, at the back of the client's skull, necessarily while the client writes, in red ink on a roll of toilet paper, a poem entitled "Poem with a Gun to Its Head"; (5) that the work in question must abide by at least three of the following terms; (6) that the client must include, at least once in the poem, and in the following rank and file, the words "only rifles have souls";

(7) that the client's childhood friend, Nicholas J. Frandsen, while aiming a loaded AK-47 at the client's skull and wearing his fatigues, may feel himself moved to speak the following words in rank and file: "you must work from yourself, like working a scarf of dried blood from a thistle, a morsel of sour bread that casts the world in copper light, a kind of penny-light that announces to the world, quote, 'I will meet death unafraid,'" whereupon the client's childhood friend, a platoon sergeant of the U.S. Marine Corps, will remember the following terms of his two tours of Iraq; (8) the tedium, the mess tent, the chemical burns, the gun cleaning, the new fish, the rank, the sleeping in holes, the fraternal, the smart-alecky, the choruses, the trap music, the religious boredom, the ague, the commandant, you kill or be killed, the flight home, a sunburnt cheek, hysterical laughter, the birthday cards, the gun cleaning, and whereupon the client's childhood friend will be moved to (9) fire a single round of 7.62 x 39 mm ammunition into the skull of the client, necessarily on the grounds that (10) for Nicholas J. Frandsen, "irreconcilable" & "incontrovertible" are no longer words in the English language but rather the phantom pain of

two claws, most likely those of a bear, impaled on either side of his ribcage, and what will hereafter be referred to as "the irreconcilable claw" will be described on the following terms; (11) that the governing body that started the war in which I fought is the same governing body whose morals and laws I took an oath to protect and simultaneously the same governing body who will decide, upon receipt of this appeal, if a poet who is free to make art in the United States, necessarily because of men and women who serve in the armed forces, will be allocated the same government money I received, the difference being the allocation of his government money will fund a work entitled "Poem With a Gun to Its Head," a work in which I am necessarily cast because of time I served as a platoon sergeant in the U.S. Marine Corps, simultaneously a role in which I dress in the same fatigues I wore while enlisted in the U.S. Marine Corps, and hold an automatic rifle to the temple of my childhood friend so as to force him to create art, which is to say these facts are "irreconcilable" insofar as they pierce me away from the world in which I live, and what will hereafter be known as "the incontrovertible claw" will be described on the following terms; (12) that it is undeniable and indisputable that I learned to disarm, dismember, and kill human beings in order to defend the rights of artists to create works in which I am cast in the not unaggressive role of someone who will be taunted and also tested, necessarily because of my training in disarming, dismembering, and killing human beings, taunted not only to murder a poet out of irreconcilable disgust but also to murder my childhood friend because it is undeniable that I fought a war in order to allow him the freedom to create this work, which is to say I find these facts "incontrovertible" insofar as they pierce me away from the world in which I live and cannot be removed, whereupon (13) as stated above, the client's childhood friend, Nicholas J. Frandsen, will be moved to fire a single round of 7.62 x 39 mm ammunition into the skull of the client, whereupon (14) the work will be completed and the above-named warehouse will be demolished by an anonymous third party (hereafter known as "the demolisher"), who will destroy the warehouse by means of finding a dead-man's switch in the woods and pushing a red button, whereupon (15) any persons whosoever who find themselves in the position of witnessing this work entitled "Poem with a

Gun to Its Head" (and hereafter known as "the audience") will be given the option, by way of detailed instructions written by the client prior to the execution of the work, of robbing the nearest Bank of America at gunpoint and demanding the sum total of $90,000, which will effectively cancel all execution of this work, barring an act of god, and be divided among the client and Nicholas J. Frandsen as follows; (16) $45,000 to the client, necessarily on the grounds that this is the same amount of money that he is proposing to be paid for creation of the work entitled "Poem with a Gun to Its Head," and about which he states, quote, "it's more or less the number at which I price my life," and this is subsequently the same amount of money, before taxes, on which the client survived for one calendar year in 2016, and thereafter $45,000 to Nicholas J. Frandsen, as this is the amount of money the client believes the United States government still owes his childhood friend, and furthermore the client is fairly convinced that, quote, "if it means not having to make art in the United States of America, any honest person can live off a meager sum and be happy."

SORROW IS MY OWN YARD

What I worship both wartime & pax in low country

is sweat

& pay-dirt & death to the tea tax

& any day I want now I can say to my captors

tomorrow, you watch

we'll be the end of America

& history with horseshoes for eyes

with ice in her beard

with shoes filled with salt

it's history who'll prove me a shrewd man

It's history who'll pin the wine-dark heart

to my breastplate for free

•

But miles off, miles off tonight in the lemon trees

(the newspapers

catch in the branches some nights like a straw bale will

catch in the threshing machine)

will my captors permit me to listen for my obituary

Will it rustle far off in the footnotes at the end of low country

Will they permit my life

to write my life its obituary

Defeaters, defeaters, I am living tonight

for that rustling

I am living tonight for the threshing machine

Forever I am living in springtime when my life's like my tea:

I want to take it in her garden

I want to take it black

I want to take it, defeaters

among my lawfully wedded's lemon trees

LAGUARDIA

Not long ago

it's a taxi

when the driver

says which way

do you feel

like taking

I say you sadsack

malingering

cunt I snort it

to be honest

it's a red eye .

meant for Florida

to toast Lisa

it's American

Airlines a gift

to the corporate

shill in the mirror

for my birthday

& us flooring

past Dutch Kills

(I have no idea

what the town

is like to live in

but it made me

think my people

must've been

assassins, spies

or honestly

it's another hole

probably named

for butchers

slash thieves

with goatees

& epaulets

who struck rich

from beaver kill

& pelt sales)

when I tell him

I'm poems

for a living

& god sent

me to die

in the backstreets

because yes

the argument is

there's still America

we haven't found

yet in America

he says you mean

you're telling me

there's a book

you can get out

of this death trap

furthermore kid

you look like a guy

who hates sweat

but it's the dead

of red August

& I can't help

but notice kid

you're flying

he shouts this

TO THE *SUN*

SHINE STATE

my profession

not that you

asked he

says it's nice

but the poor life

it's starting

to get to me

you got any

smokes he says

I knew a girl

survived two years

erotic dancing

in this absinthe

lounge he

shouts it like this

IN VER-SAILS

it was my life

I'd do a Woody

Guthrie hobo

routine he says

& hopping them

box cars

I want to scrape

your mustache

off I tell him

& run your belly

through with

a trench knife

next I wear

your skin into

the terminal

next I flee

to the bread belt

you look like

a man I can't help

but notice who'd

make a good

disguise & no one

will question me

another sadsack

malingering white

trash marauder

with a social

security number

his mustache

it twitches once

like a beetle

he says remember

when you leave

the city kid

you still have to go

live in America

TELÉMAKOS

When you meet yourself

the weird upon

you old knife

this fish-breeding

sea upon you

old knife & father

with spume

in our beard

you will know

which one of us gets filled

When you meet yourself

the weird upon

you old knife

this fish-breeding

sea upon you

old knife & father

with spume

in our beard

you will know

which one of us gets filled

RED SMEAR

They say people come to this pest house to find out whose kingdom they live in.

And that peeling you hear, says the red woman.

That's the creek bed disgracing you in every language it speaks tonight.

Which tonight the red woman tells us is three.

The tongue of the fever shed, the tongue of the quarantine, the tongue of the lazaretto.

And see her sucking the salt from her broom handle now, the red woman.

She says neither you nor your people drove a stake through your kingdom to settle it.

But it's true a buffalo limped through here one night with an arrow wound.

And you swarmed to this creek bed where she lay bleeding out, says the red woman.

And that scintilla of blood that fell from that animal's muzzle.

That red smear in the water was the first child to be born in your kingdom.

And see her sucking the plaque from her teeth now, the red woman.

Beneath a windfall of arrows your child was blown loose from the herd, she says.

Red Smear you named her, and you placed a red spoon in her hand.

Your people said *build*, they said build us a tunnel to heaven.

And in full view of heaven you began building the barrier that surrounded her.

And your barrier, says the red woman, your barrier it took many deaths.

And see her sopping the cracks from her lips now, the red woman.

Year one in your kingdom your child grew until her knees split the barrier.

And so you made for the forest to cut wood for more planks, says the red woman.

And you made for the smith to melt ore for more bolts, says the red woman.

And you made for the distillery to ply the builders with rotgut, she says.

And so you made for the apothecary to poultice the wounds of the builders.

And see her lancing the boil from her chin now, the red woman.

But year two in your kingdom, your child grew until her skull split the heavens.
And it was you who ran to the church for more gods, says the red woman.
And your gods ran to their gods, who ran to their gods, says the red woman.
And in full view of heaven it was gods begging gods for more heavens.
And the next life stared back at you dumbly with its sewed-shut mouth and no eyes.

And see her dressing her sores in the false dawn now, the red woman.

Grew do you hear me, your child grew until you couldn't tell her apart from the world.
And the next day your people, they couldn't remember whose kingdom they lived in.
"Where she ends and where the barrier begins, I can't say," said your people.
"And where she ends and where the heavens begin, I can't say," said your gods.
You people, you gods, who in full view of heaven believed you settled your kingdoms.

And see her toasting a red handful of worms to the daybreak now, the red woman.

Your first born grew red and unrecognizable and your people grew red with your child.
Your crops grew red and your creek bed grew red and your forests.
Your barrier grew red and your heavens grew red and your sun.
Your muzzles grew red and your planks grew red and your language.
And you sang what all people sing when they can't say whose kingdom they live in.

"My first born will answer, and my question's my arrow," says the red woman.

WORKS AND DAYS

Hesiod insists his name means *the shovel*.

And this life on my spade

"it will end"

"in two acts."

ACT ONE

Before I grow up

& I die a legend to nobody

ACT TWO

I'll grow up

get poorly

& ghost-write

my brother's life story.

•

They called it 1983 when they triggered me.

And mom coughed me up—

a fist of white drugs on a patch of dead leaves in the timothy.

Supposed to be:

a child was born on this day with a badger brush in his teeth end of story.

But the badger before she is skinned

& the bristles

long after the skinning

each to each we have yearns of our own

& the brush

in my mouth it kept foaming.

•

Yes like a goat I followed a girl who drooled wine from her mouth into mine.

Life named this the new millennium, not me.

•

And the man from the Party with the bombardier look on his face & gold cheekbones

you reek he said

like a mutt

with a face that

could cook

up a fundraiser.

They called her Red Dirge their flag & they drove her stake through my chin.

And I bore her

in rivers of grain up to their podium.

I gazed out at the townies my name

on their pickets

my campaign

awareness money

hanging like mouthfuls of haggis from the citizenry's pockets.

•

(Go, let history tell you.)

•

"He didn't even have the balls to vote party line."

•

"I want to smoke me

out of me," I thundered.

"Like this name you're calling me is a rodent who's wintering

no summering

inside the fifty

dividing walls of my ancestry's body."

•

Thence I lived a short life the haunch of a joke.

(Rain, gunfire, crows).

•

Five years thence I was famously addicted to whiskey dick & for the umpteenth time in my life

when I smelled the sal volatile

I turned raw

I skinned my head on the sky & woke up in custody

& the poorly cropped

local police they're a dynasty

& they beat the classified ads from teeth like they were sifting a jewel from a feed bag.

•

No second acts in American lives

sings Hesiod

whose asshole is always bleached white as a daylily.

And no gun to go off neither.

Simply me, said my brother in the middle of his life in an elk lodge.

•

I'll never forget the telephone poles of my youth, he said.

Mudpuppies under the flagstones, he said.

And my enemies

how I loved them

when they ambushed me inside the bamboo.

•

Hesiod insists

act two

will be *fin*

when I tell you the jaws of life's what they needed

when they needed to pry a girl from the mud

with the balls

to wedlock my brother.

Problem being.

Life when you land it

is a low-paying job.

And act three'd already begun with no mud.

•

I have chosen the life of no wants, I tell them.

My house it's not even one thimble.

Jarfuls of piss

my father's

they wait

like a trust fund

stacked high

as a plateful

of haggis

down cellar.

I was sent to this village to die in this village.

Now my village

is an ingrown

hair on my dick.

It soothes me the chafing when the head lice rut in the dumpsters.

And the rednecks drive cocked

off the bridge

to the cock fights.

In this village I can hear a mosquito suck blood from the chin of a hireling.

And a hireling

suck dye from a lollipop.

You dynasty men.

You come to my door once a year & sucking your teeth with a summons.

I'll wire you

what I wired god

when god told me

"eat dust"

"& find work."

The man's not been born who can stop me from slumming.

The mayor he owes me the keys to the village.

And I'll live here the rest of my life.

THE LIKES OF YOU

Means each hour for lack of a church bell

your priest rings a hand-me-down guillotine,

and into the wood chipper falls the farmhand

who each spring instead of the cherry blossoms

blooms from the cherry trees, it means he's in league

with your town drunk, your chief of police,

it means they're reminiscing blotto tonight

about their reign of terror over the mudpuppies,

over the combine blades, over the peregrines,

and they drape their 60,000 miles of veins

like angel hair from the last of the evergreens,

it means last on the list of everything they'll never teach you

about the white trash, tax-frauding

unincorporated village that established you circa 1986

(and you won't find it in your *Want Ad Digest*)

(and you won't find it in your father's

father's *father's* farmer's almanac)

is that when your dogs die of three species of tapeworm

you hold each one by the tail like a broiler,

start counting off nine-nine-nine,

and when you're pissing into the reservoir,

when you're poisoning the city's drinking supply,

when you're cursing the mayor's new pipeline

and spray-painting "god forgives but we don't"

on the 99-cent clapboard you stole from Wickham's

and nailed to the front of your house with a chukka boot,

you throw your dogs & their seventeen bags of chow

into the west branch of the Delaware River,

it means they never teach you your brother's shadow it stinks

like the priest only worse, means your thoroughbred

with her lathered, incomplete withers

and death's French accent in her cough,

when that horse dies of wet brain it means you buy all

the worst liquor you can find in the legion hall

and dump her into the Delaware River.

Generations, generations you'll hear them bragging

about that backwoods piss-drunk horse funeral:

"he wore out the skins on his hanger-toms

and tossed each one like a hogshead of wine

into the west branch of the Delaware River,"

means the river floods for the 17th time in 10 years,

it means bloated and with four hooves pointed at god

you positively ID the cow that won the blue ribbon

at the Delaware County Fair floating dead

down the west branch of the Delaware River,

it means what they won't teach you in the Academy

is how each drink you drink is the last fuck you'll fuck

and it means the last slash on the tallied-up list of everything

they never intended to teach you about your heritage,

like least of all how grateful you ought to be

that there's only this one world left for you to die in.

GLASNOST

But how do I get rid of a body.   Instructions for scrambling a frequency.

And what are the jobs near the White House.   Best practices for smothering a cry.

But who cooks the president's breakfast.   And how do I get rid of a body.

Instructions for breaking a chokehold.   But when do I disable the firewall.

Best practices for forging a signature.   And what room does the president sleep in.

But how do I get rid of a body.   Instructions for filing off serial numbers.

And where is the silent alarm located.   Best practices for taking a bullet.

But what explodes when you touch it.   And how do I get rid of a body.

Instructions for absorbing a blow.   But where can I purchase a hollow-point.

Best practices for soldering a wound.   And what time does the president eat.

But how do I get rid of a body.   Instructions for detaining a prisoner.

And how many yards to the door.   Best practices for obtaining a death certificate.

But how tall is the fence that surrounds it.   And how do I get rid of a body.

Instructions for manufacture of tear gas.   But how do I erase my identity.

Best practices for building a dead-switch.   And how far without breaking a bone.

But how do I get rid of a body.   Instructions for bugging a board room.

And where can I locate the safety.   Best practices for home-cooking napalm.

But where do I purchase a firearm.   And how do I get rid of a body.

Instructions for strapping on kevlar.   But who are the names on the watch list.

Best practices for squeezing the trigger.   And how do I clear a room.

But how do I get rid of a body.   Instructions for securing a blindfold.

And how many years for treason.   Best practices for beating a death warrant.

But how close without tripping a wire.   And how do I get rid of a body.

LIVERY

When my handlers

they pile me

into the black chevrolet

I may ash

but my money's

what'll melt

holes in the upholstery.

It's my broker

Old Hickory

who'll claim what I need to claim for me.

Who'll handle

the wheel

like a mule left out in the rain.

It's his job to see that my flanks steam.

When I spend him

he oversees how I bay.

Have you ever sang "my love" inside a black chevrolet

"must be a brand"

"a kind of"

"blind love"

(cue rain)

(it's the job of the rain to disfigure

what it can't wash away)

like my money inside my billfold inside a black chevrolet.

When I ash

it's like hearing my life pass

inside a key change that's the scourge of the American music industry.

Or like hearing

my life

but my life's

cashing my life in at the penny arcade.

Have you ever sang "maybe millions" inside a black chevrolet

"of people"

"pass by"

"but they all disappear"

"from view."

It's the job of

Old Hickory

to make sure that he brokers the rain.

It's the job of the ash in the lanterns down Ashland Place

to make sure that

they light us an entranceway to the sea.

I don't want my life

(it's the job of

my life to say)

to knot like the hair of Old Hickory

which breaks

when it crests

& burns more berserk than the sea.

It's the job of the keys in a black chevrolet

to change hands from broker to broker.

And mine to ash

& smell life disfigure.

"But I only have eyes"

"for you."

ARCHILOCHOS

There's a sergeant who bends the notes to his life on a kettledrum,

what he calls love I call *kriegspiel*,

gah, I've tasted this kind of workmanship with the klaxons,

his showmanship under klieg lights,

his name should be spelled like a criminal broke through the wall of it,

a name like Sergeant Petraeus

(literally, "a country that can't quit pissing out kidney stones")

or don't you wish his Grossmutter

was possessed of the balls to name him Here Come the Lions,

and she'd call out his name like his name's an x-rated splatter film,

and she'd drip-paint his name on the terra incognita,

wherever her grandson's pink flag

wasn't staked, staked on his map of the world circa 1510,

meanwhile I work eight jobs

gah, I've no leave, zero maternity, it's with poetry I bring down the state.

It's me not him, not him,

who'll make this country famous by dying here.

With my weapon I breaded my family,

blotto I slept with my weapon,

weapon I out berserk'd the berserkers with, *gah*

I knelt inside your war and I chugged, I chugged.

But I won't tar the republic's children,

not for all the unspent drachma in their trust funds, *gah*

I won't confetti their graves,

not when their children tell me their unborn head lice,

their forthcoming handfuls of dandruff are worth more than my spear.

Republicans are liberals too I'm afraid,

and there's no such thing as a trust fund kid on the battlefield.

All this country has left in common with me,

this jawbone of an ass,

gah, this country that lived how I lived and it'll die how I'll die,

with my tongue in your mouth

like a buck in the swear jar,

yes I've heard them calling me Ancient Latrine, full of the kind of mealy,

malnourished shit, they say, that's unfit for labor,

unless labor means landing your name on the government watch list.

Pretty soon, forget *warrior,*

they'll have to start digging me up and calling me sergeant.

Dollar after dollar after dollar would you listen to me cuss.

TROJAN

In the coming days my representative is coming for you with a storm worm.

Until then under no circumstances should you contact my representative.

Regardless of whose representative sends my representative to your door.

I repeat the name of my representative is not red storm in the white house.

I'm talking a storm worm that opens a torch that burns my whole representative.

But sources say you should blast my representative to everyone in your contacts.

For it's better to receive my representative nine dozen times than the torch.

Even if you believe my representative is named red dirge in the white house.

If my representative enters your system—your system shuts down immediately.

It's true the worst torch ever announced by the representatives is my representative.

I'm talking classified by the system as the most destructive representative ever.

But sources indicate my representative was elected to your contacts via storm worm.

And in the coming days there will be no coming back from my representative.

Even if you open the red storm that destroys the name of my representative.

TRIVIA

Did you know

68,557 days

(& still piling)

in the jaundiced

canvasback heart

of the Capitol

at 11:59 PM

& since 1845

(the year dropsy

claimed Old

Hickory whilst

a farmhand

lifted him out

of his beloved

African walnut

barrel-chair

& whereupon

a black sunflower

began swiftly

growing out of

his gallbladder)

the ghosts of

the ghosts of

the ghosts of

a generation of

strike-breakers

drunks & for-hire

rabble rousers

swear in Andrew

Jackson on a 500-

year-old first

edition Oxford

Bible & Rocky

Mountain wood-

ticks skittering

out of his eye-

holes & shaking

their castanets

yes & clucking

their tongues

it's split pea soup

boiling out of

his mouth holes

& whereupon

the mob on

their shoulders

they hoist Old

Hickory in his

beloved African

barrel-chair

burn the White

House anterooms

to the plinths

& whereupon

the Party blesses

a barrel of 313-

year-old corn

whiskey rumored

to be seasoned

with the scalp of

a magistrate of

the Old World

beheaded they

say for treason

& whereupon

the new head of

state & his acolytes

crawl the riot

to the lawn of

the now-mayor's

brownstone so

as not to destroy

the beloved walnut

barrel-chair but

more pressing

is the establishment

of an historical

exemplar for

these coming

days of uncertainty

quotidian strife

& hysteria

REAGANOMICS

WHO'LL PROVE ME THE SHREWD MAN

IT'S YOUR HISTORY

ON HER BIB AND TWO DAQUIRIS

IN HER BEARD ZERO STAINS

AND HISTORY WITH CRUMBS

WILL BE THE END OF AMERICANS

TOMORROW, YOU WATCH

AT HOME IN YOUR LIVING ROOMS

I CAN SAY TO YOU FOLKS

BECAUSE ANY DAY I WANT NOW

49 RECORDINGS OF SNOW

In days as yellow as the day's first piss is

I field what I field

like I'm fielding the question of which field won't survive itself

& the very field

which won't survive itself

is my questioner.

This very love in the straw I smell trying to patent me is my questioner.

This very spider's a father

(Latin: *hacklemesh weaver*)

who burgles his way through the slit in my lips when I'm blackout in winter

& canine to molar

weaves

his resignation letter

& tenders his absence

addressed to the son strapped inside the cradleboard strapped to his back

is my questioner.

Spiderling of mine I've been to so many people I can't say if I'll break into again.

Quoth the weaver.

It's nights as scared of themselves alone in a field with a man

as a man alone in a field with the night is

when the color of my love for the ones who spit on their love of my colors

I dye myself.

I crave the missing

persons stay

missing & venture

a religion in

which one is holy

if one never

letters the names.

If one never patents the very smell of the love that's still after the rights to me.

Said Dickinson.

Doing her best Ronald-Reagan's-ash-heap-of-history-speech impression.

To the lions

to the capital L

& into the history of the jaws of life she spoke this

& sewed shut

the eyes of the world which lays eggs in the eyes of the polis.

ARMA VIRUMQUE CANO, they'll tell you.

This soldiery of horseflies who're prisoner on the back of a hacklemesh weaver

who according to legend

will trespass into my mouth when I'm blackout midwinter.

In days as false as the day's first dawn is

I war what I war

like I'm warring against the question of which war lives the longest

& the very war

which won't live the longest

is longest.

ARMA VIRUMQUE CANO, they'll tell you.

And when they ask you what I was like don't show them my broadaxe.

DESTRUDO

But what if I tried a wasp's

eating frosting

off my swoll bottom lip

and my sex

won't let me down from the lemon tree.

What if I tried a mashed-up fist

of $2,000

bride's pye

wedding cake's in my windbreaker.

What if I tried mashing it into my face when I gave away my daughter.

What if I tried the father

daughter dance

& the voice of a cowboy singing *I'm cleaning this gun.*

But nothing laughs.

What if I tried dementia's the drum

which makes me

the orchestra pit

& it'll beat my nemesis

so long as I scrape on a tux & disgrace my music in front of her.

But nothing works.

I shall call these my Nothing Works.

In this year of our.

Anno domini.

I'm a man who won't climb down

pathetic you hear me lord

from his lemon tree

& smashing cake into his maw sans idolatry.

Because *aroused.*

Aroused is the failed word.

Not for all the tea leaves I would eat from the lord's teeth

does it begin to unearth the mortar

nor the fortress of my sanity.

All of which

I want demolition'd.

Like when I work my sanity into the loose

summer labia

of this flower boy

without

his chrysanthemum

what I hear's death pronouncing my name when his petals say thank you.

Or I'm demolitioning god

that I was not named Gabriel.

In falsetto in

c minor in

death's brogue

in escrow

I'm death who karaokes the national anthem.

NEUTRALITY

D   SCH   B   's F   S B .   F P   MS,   *M*   *C*   *B*   *CD*,   S P   B   SH   D

[*the interrogators inform the detainee one morning that he can earn a bucket if he cooperates*]

B   S   S B   S   2014.   S F   D S   F H   's   S   D   D B   S

[*mistakes the director strongly believes should be expected in a business filled with uncertainty*]

B   *P*   *S &*   S   D B *S*   *V*   C   S   "   G   DB   G F   S   B   H

[*insofar as our budget is we either tell our story or we get eaten there is no middle ground*]

S   DS   F   C   H   S H   C D   S P   S   F   S   H   's G   ."   H   S

[*because it's unclear what the impact will be, not because we believe we can improve the country*]

H   S   PP   D   *P*   ,   H   S ,   B   S   *V*   ,   F   C ,   B   MB,   *V*   ,

[*with a bottle of that unknown pink solution resting on wooden beams surrounded by buckets*]

J B   ,   D   S   H   . H   S   C   M   P   F   H   M   C   D ,

[*may have been slandered by 26 rivals who were wrongfully detained but could not be ignored*]

H   S   S   H   H   CH   J   B   D   G S   S,   D   D   S   H   P   P   S   S.   2015,

[*detainee states in his autobiography that a box with the dimensions of a coffin was approved*]

P   C   D   S   H   S   S   C   D B   ,   V   G   C   D *C*' S   *G*   .

[*spent the rest of the day with the white curtain that separates his room from the interrogators*]

AVELLINO

Went looking for death in these pews I said death

does a good job I hear

(when death has to)

& swinging death's thurible

& saddles

death's junco

I said follow her death

her stench

from jonquil to jonquil

.

Went scrounging for coins in these troughs I said death

what's the damage

how much

do I owe you

for delivering my lady of mange

her onionskin bible

(death's cough

knocked the pages out

like a fistful

of shale

through her window)

& her veils

cry the spaniels

the wind stole our lady's veils

•

In her hair death went sniffing for two fistfuls of amaranth:

    Said you cry heathen cry you.

        •

That's cat gut

death strings

in his guitarra de golpe, you heathen

(& little stray

you'll sing too

when death plucks you)

        •

In her hair death went sniffing for two fistfuls of amaranth:

    Said you cry heathen cry you.

        •

Went looking for death in these juts I said death

if the shale miners

surface

with lye in their eyes

& we disown the last saint we prayed to

(death's lamp

death leaves sputtering)

& we each one disown

the light

inside the room we last lit you

(& the wick

spurns the flame spurns)

do you fill

my mouth death

with frankincense too

•

In her hair death went sniffing for two fistfuls of amaranth:

Said you cry heathen cry you.

DITCH LILY

So this is my dénouement.

I meet my enemy I kick his head across the field.

I meet the foreman

and kick his head across the field.

I forge my father's signature

on the face of the ditch lily.

I meet the ruler of life I kick her head across the field.

So this was for me in the offing.

They say each day your war drums'll begin me.

I'll brush your grackle of silence

I'll oil the wings.

I'll limp to my basin and wash.

I did not want to draw out your leaders

by banging a trash can.

Nor congratulate you on our death.

But the dead are ongoing

they dance to *American Bandstand*.

And the cops are ongoing they kick handfuls of mother's red hair in my face.

Didn't I murmur three centuries?

Didn't I hang myself with a madwoman's beard?

And this is the ditch where I terminus?

Will someone please tell me what are the four pillars.

I meet my betrothed I kick her head across the field?

I meet my boss

and kick her head across the field?

I hand you the shears

and the tyrants they line up to watch?

What if I say I've come for my personals.

Not on your life say the tyrants.

And the names that scroll down the black

at the end of your life.

We want to be *those* names they tell me.

So this is my dénouement.

This drink in my suitcase.

Do you see it?

Frisk harder.

This drink in my suitcase is a dream I won't have of you.

A dream you won't have of yourself.

DARK-EYED JUNCO WAS HER NAME

But a world will begin a world do you hear me a world.

A world it will always begin

when your hostiles

will not let you stay dead.

And this next generation of hostiles

with ice in their beards

with horseshoes for eyes

with shoes filled with salt.

They prowl until they find your kingdom in disrepair.

And beside you lay husbands who danced themselves to death.

And beside them lay hostiles who danced themselves to death.

And cries this next generation of men who surround you:

"Need sustenance."

Like this

the world began once again for the woman behind the barrier.

Began once again

past the barrier

& her work

was prowling

for apricots

& the cockscomb

when it sang

the red song

of her prowling

she tore out

the cockscomb

with both fists

to quiet it.

So gathering roots

was her work

So gathering oats

was her work

So gathering pits

was her work

& the world

for a time

it hung

from these hooks.

But this time the world it wouldn't live through her she said.

Infidel world

with its shotpouch of sun

its cockscomb

& half-cocked agenda

in which the sun once a day climbs the battlement

while the woman

is prowling for apricots

& the sweat the sun makes soak through her sun dress

is the alcohol

of legend known throughout the barrier'd kingdom

first by its maiden name

which is rotgut.

A world will begin in which dying of crumbs is your honor.

And to drink

god's swill

is the privilege

of hostiles

& better than

death itself

yes & luckier.

"At sunrise when I'm dying of crumbs I can smell her leak alcohol," says the first hostile.

"It's like auditioning for the part of myself."

"At noon when I'm dying of waste I can taste her leak alcohol," says another.

"It's like auditioning for the part of myself."

And all together the hostiles say:

"The rotgut that sweats from the woman behind the barrier."

"It's like auditioning for the part of myself."

So she sweats

for the youngest

boy first

wrings her dress

at his lips.

"A world will begin"

says the youngest

"don't misword"

"what I'm prophesying"

"a world will begin"

"by his feathers"

"I will drag god"

"out of heaven"

"& yes my love"

"long ago was the bird"

"the one with the"

"dark eyes the one"

"they call junco"

& he ties a gray string 'round her wrist.

A world began

"do not steal away"

said the hostiles

"do not rest"

"not until we"

"afford us"

"our chance"

"to rancid"

"ourselves"

"with your sweat."

And this pile of mason jars surrounding her pallet each night.

And a pile of hostiles

in the cockscomb each night.

And messing themselves

which is food for the cockscomb.

And singing a red song to her each night is the cockscomb.

Night the gaslight of death

swims like koi up the wall.

In packs long ago

it was hostiles who

settled her

& they sang

while they stalked

on their drunks

through the blurred

fields of rotgut.

Long ago in a world where the sun makes of you the world's harvest.

So she sweats

for the oldest

man last

lays her palms

on his lips.

"A world will begin"

says the oldest

"in the likeness of"

"this daughter"

"I dream I fathered"

"so young she"

"sweats through"

"this world & yet"

"what she can't"

"rid herself of"

"in the sunlight"

"is what she'll"

"love most"

"in this infidel world."

Like the cockscomb's red song in the night when the sweat leaves the world.

Like these silvering leaves of the cockscomb that lose her the world.

A world will begin

with no choice.

One morning your hostiles will not let you stay dead.

The next day the sun

the sun

incites rotgut in you.

And the next day a bird pulls a nightcrawler out of the earth like she's told.

And the next day a low wind blows through a patch of dead leaves in the timothy.

And the sun in its shame.

Without ceremony.

With no war left to prove it the sun eliminates itself from the throne.

Sun will not rise.

Sun will not work.

Sun will not battle.

And the day will be finished now.

Because the light will be finished now.

And the rotgut is finished now.

Because the sweat will be finished now.

And the hostiles are finished now.

Because the harvest is finished now.

And the shotpouch is finished now.

Because the sun will be finished now.

And the world will be finished now.

Because the woman is finished now.

And now when

the cockscomb

it sings its red

song she watches

it worsen

with time.

A world will begin.

A world do you hear me a world.

And this last jar of rotgut she leaves at the foot of her pallet.

Long ago past the battlements

in the kingdom behind the barrier

it was men

who smelled her

leak alcohol.

This apricot they found on the floor of the earth was not easy to live through.

Now hear them whetting

their war clubs

tonight in the unerring black.

And their whetting so loud it's like

a silent film of cicadas

& crawling over each other's backs to harvest the willow tree's xylem.

They sing "death"

"or the last jar"

"there will be"

"no third road."

Daybreak and no light to speak of.

Now hear a generation begin to churn

in the unerring black.

"I am felled."

"Take my hand."

"I will war"

"till the world"

"where you war"

"falls beneath you."

"I am felled."

"Help me stanch."

"Were we men?"

"I am felled."

"Bring me mother."

"We were men."

"We were crumbs."

"Take my hand."

"I will war."

"Help me stanch."

"Till the world"

"where you war"

"from its hooks"

"hangs me cold."

"I am felled."

"Were we men?"

"I am felled."

"Take my hand."

"We were dust."

"I am felled."

"I will war."

"Bring me mother."

"We were drunks."

"Till the world."

"Bring me mother."

"Where you war."

"Take my hand."

"We were crumbs."

"I am felled."

"Bring me mother."

You'll say—

they must really love her

to savage themselves

like they do?

A world will begin a world do you hear me a world.

Long ago

past the barrier

did she grieve

for a world

for the hostiles

who savaged

their own

generation

to drink her.

But will she place a silvering leaf on the face of each one tonight in the cockscomb.

ACKNOWLEDGMENTS

Thanks to the editors of the following journals and anthologies in which these poems first appeared:

The Academy of American Poets: "C'est la guerre"
Ambit: "Neutrality," "Telémakos," "Trivia"
American Poetry Review: "Archilocos," "Poem with a Gun to Its Head"
The Awl: "Works and Days"
The Baffler: "Sorrow Is My Own Yard"
Bat City Review: "This Neverender"
Boston Review: "Fifteen Answers of the King to His Questioners"
The Brooklyn Rail: "49 Recordings of Snow," "Ditch Lily"
The Cortland Review: "Destrudo"
Dreginald: "Livery"
Fence: "Glasnost"
Guernica: "Nachtmusik"
Hyperallergic: ".GIF"
Iowa Review: "Trébuchet"
Interrupture: "LaGuardia"
Kenyon Review: "The Likes of You"
LIT: "Coyote Tactics"
The New Yorker: "Chorus"
Noncannon Press: "Avellino"
Pleiades: "Russets"
Poetry: "The Dancing Plague," "Cold Open"
Yalobusha Review: "Interns"

"Fifteen Answers of the King to His Questioners" also appears in *Privacy Policy: The Anthology of Surveillance Poetics* (Black Ocean), edited by Andrew Ridker.

"The Dancing Plague," "Interns," "C'est la guerre," and "Fifteen Answers of the King to His Questioners" were also included in *Trench Mouth*, an EP of recorded poems released by Black Cake Records in 2014.

With love and gratitude to the following people: Emily Skillings, Frank Bidart, Daniel Borzutzky, Kevin Prufer, Tyler Weston Jones, Caitlin Kaufman, Soren Stockman, Todd

Colby, Rob Spillman, Travis Meyer, Melissa Broder, Wendy Xu, Micah Gertzog,
Claire Donato, Jeff T. Johnson, Anna Moschovakis, Tianna Kennedy, Sunnie Joh,
Mary Skinner, and everyone at Bushel, Katherine Sullivan, Don Share, Timothy Donnelly,
Lynn Melnick, Bethany Snead, Jon Davies, and everyone at University of Georgia Press,
Brian Blanchfield, my family, Monica Ferrell, Lee Schlesinger, Bill Wadsworth, Zach Whitney,
Jessamee Sanders, Shawnee Sanders, Natalie Eilbert, Dolan Morgan, Matthew Zingg, Jay Silva,
Emmanuel Cruz, Kevin Dobbins, and everyone at Suburbia, Allyson Paty, Anna Janiszewski,
Salt Madeo, Cait Barrick, Marshall Scheuttle, Robert Ostrom, Sarah V. Schweig, Tom Healy,
André Nafis-Sahely, Meghan DellaCrosse, Sarah Gerard, Zachary Pace, Noah Burton,
Conrad Lochner, John Rufo, Sean D. Henry-Smith, Zoe Hitzig, Marya Spence,
Nat Baldwin, Mike Ireland, Karrie Cornell, Elizabeth Zuba, Anthony Madrid,
Nina Puro, Jordan Debor, Melinda Small, and Peter Meyer.

Thanks as well to the Millay Colony for the Arts and Oregon State University,
where several of the poems in this book were written and edited.

NOTES

The unattributed epigraph (p. 1) is partly composed of lines from Albert Speer's "Theory of Ruin Value" and Thomas McGrath's *Letter to an Imaginary Friend*.

"Fifteen Answers of the King to His Questioners" is an adaptation of an anonymous Serbian folk poem interspersed with language from President Obama's press junkets on surveillance.

"Coyote Tactics" is based on a list of "watch out situations" published in a survival manual for wildfire fighters by the Colorado Fire Camp.

One translation of the phrase "C'est la guerre" is *that's the war*.

"This Neverender" is a collaboration with Osip Mandelstam, who died in the Gulag in 1938.

"Cold Open" quotes and slightly misquotes from the INXS song "Don't Change."

"Russets" was written in collaboration with philosopher and poet Travis Holloway.

In "Poem with a Gun to Its Head," the phrase "only rifles have souls" is quoted from Carol Cosman's English translation of Albert Camus's short story "The Renegade."

"Sorrow Is My Own Yard" takes its title from the first line of William Carlos Williams's poem "The Widow's Lament in Springtime."

"LaGuardia" is for Kirill Medvedev. The poem also quotes a line from Sergei Yesenin.

"Glasnost" is based, in part, on a list of phrases that have landed U.S. citizens on government watch lists when googled.

"Livery" quotes lyrics from "I Only Have Eyes for You" by the Flamingos.

"Archilochos" is an adaptation of a poem by the seventh-century Greek soldier-poet Archilochos.

"Destrudo" quotes from the Rodney Atkins song "Cleaning This Gun."

"Trojan" is based on a spam e-mail sent to several New York City workplaces in 2014.

The erased lines in "Neutrality" are lines from the author's bio at the time, written in a font called Times Sans Neutrality (created by artist Ben Sisto), which does not contain any of the letters in the words "network neutrality"; the bracketed lines are fragments from the CIA Torture Report.

"Avellino" is a collaboration with Federico García Lorca, who was shot in the Fuente Grande in 1936.